[II]

95TH CONGRESS, 1ST SESSION . . . . SENATE DOCUMENT 95–94

Acceptance of the

Statue of
Senator Ernest Gruening

PRESENTED BY THE
STATE OF ALASKA

✿

PROCEEDINGS IN THE ROTUNDA
UNITED STATES CAPITOL

October 5, 1977

UNITED STATES GOVERNMENT PRINTING OFFICE
WASHINGTON : 1978

The great experiment begun so daringly and so hopefully two centuries ago, that great legacy bequeathed to us by the patriots of that day, and whose bicentennial we are to celebrate three years hence, is too precious and priceless to be destroyed . . . The rest of the nation needs to follow the example and recapture the courage of those—past and present—who inculcated and preserved the spirit of free men which has guided and galvanized America . . . Along with our basic freedoms to speak, to write, to think as we please, must also be freedom from fear. Men are not really free if they have to wonder whether they are. Thus believing, and acting accordingly, we shall win this battle and make the America we love happen again.

Ernest Gruening
Many Battles, 1973

Statue Presented by the People of Alaska

HONORABLE JAY S. HAMMOND, Governor
HONORABLE LOWELL THOMAS, JR., Lieutenant Governor
HONORABLE JOHN L. RADER, President, Alaska Senate
HONORABLE HUGH MALONE, Speaker, Alaska House of
Representatives
JEAN MACKIN, Chairman, Alaska State Council on the Arts

Contents

Program for Unveiling

Ernest Gruening Statue: George R. Anthonisen, Sculptor
Rotunda, U.S. Capitol, October 5, 1977, 11:00 a.m.

Concert 10:30–11:00 a.m.
The National Symphony Brass Quintet

Master of Ceremonies, George Sundborg, Administrative Assistant to Senator Gruening.

Presentation of Colors, Joint Armed Forces Color Guard.

"The Star Spangled Banner", U.S. Army Band.

Welcome, Gladys Reckley, President, Alaska State Society.

Presentation of Statue, Douglas Riggs, Special Counsel and Administrative Assistant to the Governor of Alaska.

"Ernest Gruening", Honorable Gaylord Nelson, U.S. Senator from Wisconson.

Unveiling of Statue, Dorothy Gruening.

Family Response, Hunt Gruening.

Acceptance of Statue, Honorable Ted Stevens, U.S. Senator from Alaska; Honorable Mike Gravel, U.S. Senator from Alaska; Honorable Don Young, U.S. Congressman from Alaska.

"Alaska's Flag", U.S. Army Band.

Postlude, The National Symphony Brass Quintet.

Reception following in Room S207, The Capitol

[1]

Proceedings

GEORGE SUNDBORG. Ladies and gentlemen, may I have your attention. Would you please rise for the presentation of the colors and the playing of the national anthem.

GEORGE SUNDBORG. You may be seated. My name is George Sundborg. I was Administrative Assistant to Senator Ernest Gruening for the ten years he served in the United States Senate and an assistant of his for some years previous to that when he was the Governor of Alaska when Alaska was a territory. And, because of this association I have the honor today to be the Master of Ceremonies at this event.

The first item on our program will be a welcome from Gladys Reckley, President of the Alaska State Society. Miss Reckley.

GLADYS RECKLEY. Members of the Gruening family, distinguished guests, ladies and gentlemen. It is my pleasure to welcome you on behalf of the Alaska State Society in Washington, but it was the people of Alaska who invited you here to join in honoring the late Senator Ernest Gruening. The people of Alaska, through the State Legislature, elected to honor Senator Gruening by placing a statue here in the United States Capitol. This is an important and historic occasion for our state. Each state is permitted to place only two statues in the U.S. Capitol, and in placing this statue today in the Capitol Alaska has made its final choice of the kind of man, the deeds and the service its people want remembered. If it is true that the character of a people is portrayed by the men and women they choose to honor, then the ceremony today is as much a tribute to all Alaskans as it is to Senator Gruening.

[3]

It seems quite appropriate that the Gruening statue will be here in the Capitol, recognizing Alaska's contribution of leadership and statesmanship to the nation. As an adopted son, Senator Gruening began the all-out crusade that brought Alaska into the union of states. He had been an advocate of home rule as the Director of Interior Department's Division of Territories and Island Possessions. Mr. Gruening's long association with Alaska began with his appointment in 1938 to the Alaska International Highway Commission. The following year he was appointed Governor of Alaska and reappointed twice until 1953. In preparation for statehood, Alaska, in 1956, elected its first senators on a provisional basis, and Senator Gruening was one of them. In 1958 he was elected Senator and drew the four-year term. He won re-election in 1962, serving through 1968. He brought to the Senate the inspired leadership and vitality that had marked his earlier career. Senator Gruening correctly perceived the issues, and he had the courage of his convictions. In those tumultuous middle '60's he became one of the first critics of the Vietnam war. It was here as a Washington reporter that I first met Senator Gruening. I waited with several other reporters to interview him following his vote against the Gulf of Tonkin resolution that expanded the war powers of the President. Senator Gruening had a full understanding of the role of the press. Having been a reporter and an editor before beginning his public service, he answered reporters' questions with great clarity, and there was a mutual respect. Senator Gruening proved how many useful lives one man can live. And, there is a definite message from his example for us today: You have to get interested, get well informed, step out and speak out.

Welcome to Washington.

GEORGE SUNDBORG. Thank you, Miss Reckley. I'd like to say a few words about the group of statues known as the National Statuary Hall collection, which no longer appears exclusively in Statuary Hall. By virtue of a resolution passed in 1864 each state was invited to place in this Capitol statues of two of its eminent citizens.

[4]

Alaska is the forty-second state to contribute the second and last statue to which it is entitled. Eight states, all in the West, have thus far presented only one statue each for this collection. Until 1933 the statues were in Statuary Hall, which is down this way, as many of you are well aware; but in that old chamber where the House of Representatives met before the construction of the House wing it soon became apparent that with the addition of so many states it was becoming too crowded with statues. They were standing in there three deep, and they actually presented a hazardous condition because of the great weight on the floor. And, so, in 1933 the statues were relocated throughout the Capitol. Some of them are there, and some of them are in other positions around this wonderful and historic building.

Senator Bartlett, the other Senator from Alaska, who served here immediately following the admission of Alaska as the forty-ninth state, is represented in a statue which is in the House-connecting corridor.

The statue of Senator Gruening, after the ceremony today, will be placed in the Hall of Columns. He is one of twenty-one who will be there, and will face directly across the hall at Father Damien of Hawaii. Senator Gruening's statue will join a goodly company of the statues of men who have been in the estimation of their home states the leading citizens of this nation.

Forty-one of these men, of the ninety-two that are now represented, were members of the Congress. And, in addition to that, nine more served as delegates to the Continental Congress. They are patriots, pioneers, educators, authors. There are three Jesuit priests, an Indian chief, a king—Kamehameha of Hawaii—and many others, businessmen and so on and even the inventor of the electric refrigerator.

To mention some of the names that will instantly be familiar to you, there is Samuel Adams, Henry Clay, Sam Houston, Andrew Jackson, Robert E. Lee, George Washington, Daniel Webster and Will Rogers. And, there are four women also. One

[5]

man, General James Shields, who is in the statuary collection, was notable because he was elected a U.S. Senator from three separate states—Illinois, Minnesota and Missouri—and, of course, is the only man in our history who has that distinction. I may say that Massachusetts, in addition to Sam Adams, chose the statue of John Winthrop, and John Winthrop was an ancestor of Dorothy Gruening and, therefore, of all of the Gruenings who are here today—the son and the grandchildren.

I think that the two statues representing Alaska, the second one of which we are dedicating today, are notable for the reason that they have joined the Statuary Hall collection the soonest after the end of the lives of the two men represented of any in the entire Statuary Hall collection. Senator Bartlett's statue was unveiled here only a little more than two years after his death, and Senator Gruening's today is being unveiled and dedicated just a little over three years after his death. These men were walking these halls—they passed through this chamber, this historic place—many times in the course of their duties in Washington, D.C.

These two men—and I think it is symbolic of what Alaska's great interest is—were the two people who made statehood possible for our state. Bartlett, working in Washington, D.C.; Senator Gruening, first as Governor and then as a private citizen in Alaska.

Senator Gruening—I will not say much about him because we will have on the program in a few minutes a man who is much better able to do that than I am, but he was from the standpoint of Alaskans a patriot, a pioneer, an educator. It wasn't easy for him first of all to preach the merits of statehood to the brawling territory which he found when he went there first as Governor in 1939, but he led us, he afforded us a wonderful example. I think it would now unanimously be granted by the citizens of Alaska that his idea of statehood was the right thing for Alaska. One thing I experience very often when I travel around

[6]

Alaska is that someone will come up to me and say, "Well I opposed him for years, but the old man was right about statehood." He was called the old man by most Alaskans because he never went to Alaska to live until he was fifty-two years old, and he was 71 years old when he was elected to the United States Senate. I believe, although I haven't completed the research on this, that he is the oldest individual ever to be elected to the Congress— either the House or the Senate—for the first time at the age of 71.

Now, I am going to call on Douglas Riggs, Special Counsel and Administrative Assistant to the Governor of Alaska, to present the statue. Mr. Riggs.

DOUGLAS RIGGS. Honorable members of Congress, members of the Gruening family and ladies and gentlemen. In behalf of Governor Hammond and the people of Alaska we are very pleased to make this presentation to Congress and to the people of the United States.

Senator Gruening's contributions to Alaska were enormous. Among his most noteworthy were his commitments to Native rights and Alaskan statehood. His dynamic and persistent leadership in these two areas endeared him to the hearts of Alaskans, and formed in their minds an enduring acknowledgment for this very special person. A representation of this acknowledgment is this beautiful statue. Alaskans are proud of Senator Gruening. We are proud to make this presentation today. Thank you.

GEORGE SUNDBORG. Thank you, Mr. Riggs. I once heard Senator Gruening say—in fact, I heard him say it more than once—that in the best of all worlds Gaylord Nelson would be our President. Our next speaker is going to be the distinguished junior Senator from Wisconsin, Senator Gaylord Nelson.

SENATOR NELSON. Mr. Sundborg, members of Senator Gruening's family and friends and admirers of Senator Gruening. Fifty-three years ago Bob LaFollette, old Bob LaFollette, won

[7]

more than sixteen percent of the vote as a third-party Presidential candidate. He relied heavily on the counsel of his brilliant, 37-year-old director of national publicity, Ernest Gruening. I am sure that old Bob LaFollette would be pleased to see the statue of Ernest Gruening standing today in Statuary Hall, where the statue now stands of Senator LaFollette.

Alaska loved Senator Gruening as Wisconsin loved Senator LaFollette. The courage, integrity and conviction of both men have been an inspiration for all who knew them and what they stood for. On March 7, 1974, three and a half months before the death of Senator Gruening, I joined with four of my colleagues in a tribute to our friend. We wrote a letter placing his name in nomination for the Nobel Peace Prize. I would like to, if I may, read part of that letter to you today:

"Senator Gruening's leadership in the quest for peace spans many issues in several generations. It goes back as far as the magazine and newspaper editorials he wrote as a journalist against the gunboat diplomacy of the 1920's and against the interventions in Hawaii, the Dominican Republic and Nicaragua. It is as current as the efforts he continues now in his eighty-seventh year against steps which would heighten the danger of a more serious confrontation in Indochina. He is a man of energy, of integrity and of absolute dedication to justice and to the cause of peace. He fights tirelessly for what he believes, and we have all learned that what he believes is usually right."

Senator Gruening's death in 1974 caught us all off guard because though he was eighty-seven he was a young man. He was youthful in his thoughts and vigor, and though it seems hardly possible, his age seemed to enhance his enthusiasms rather than diminish them. As a young man Ernest Gruening enrolled in the Harvard Medical School, planning to follow his father's footsteps as a doctor. But, his broad interests and his realization that the afflictions of men and women were more than just physical carried him beyond his medicine. While still in medical school he

[8]

took a newspaper job for $15 a week. He would later serve as a newspaper and magazine editor, foreign correspondent, author, historian, diplomat, territorial governor and lobbyist for Alaskan statehood and finally United States Senator and statesman.

Senator Hubert Humphrey once described him as the twentieth century Benjamin Franklin. In the Senate Ernest Gruening was a man whose views commanded respect even though he often, very often, espoused unpopular causes. In March, 1964, five months before the Gulf of Tonkin resolution was brought before the Senate, he made the first major Senate speech calling for the United States to get out of Vietnam. In it he decried the loss of American lives in seeking vainly, he said, "to shore up self-serving, corrupt dynasts or their self-imposed successors." On that day he spoke with passion, with outrage, with sadness and with great foresight. "I consider," Senator Gruening said, "the life of one American boy worth more than this putrid mess. I consider every additional life that is sacrificed in this forlorn venture a tragedy. Some day not too distant if this sacrificing continues it will be denounced as a crime."

Few listened or understood when Senator Gruening made that prophesy, but he never gave up. He pleaded the case against our Vietnam involvement on the Senate floor, in the cloakroom, in the offices and in the great public forum. After many years—far too many years—his views took hold. This country's attitude and its policies changed.

Those concerned with world population, overpopulation, and all the problems that accompany it also owe a special debt to Senator Gruening. Early, early in this century young Ernest Gruening realized that population control was an essential step toward higher health standards and the elimination of poverty and eventually toward a more civilized and peaceful world. He was an advocate of birth control in the 1920's, when such a position was virtually unheard of. His warnings, as his warnings on the dangers of our involvement in Vietnam forty years later, were greeted with indifference or hostility.

[9]

Tiffany Gruening, who did the unveiling.

Son Hunt Gruening speaking at the unveiling.

After he was elected to the Senate he continued his crusade virtually alone. It was primarily Senator Gruening's efforts that were responsible for the creation of the Office of Population Affairs within the Department of Health, Education, and Welfare and for the appropriation of $175 million in 1963 for a pioneer program to foster birth control efforts abroad.

But, to the people of his beloved Alaska, Ernest Gruening will always be their father of statehood. It was a cause he championed as territorial governor and in the mid-1950's as the Territory's elected but unofficial Senator/lobbyist in Washington. In 1958 his efforts were rewarded when Congress voted to make Alaska the forty-ninth state. Later that year he went on to win election as one of Alaska's United States Senators. As the people of Alaska know, he carried on in the Senate the fight on their behalf against those who would exploit the State's abundant resources and destroy its magnificence.

In his book "Many Battles" Ernest Gruening defined life as a series of battles. He did not always win, but he never lost by default. Thank you.

GEORGE SUNDBORG. Thank you, Senator Nelson. Your program shows at this point that the statue will be unveiled by Dorothy Gruening. Dorothy Gruening, of course, is the widow of Ernest Gruening, but for reasons of health she was not able to join us today. She lives in Issaquah, Washington, in a home where she is cared for, close to the home of her son, Hunt Gruening, who with his family are here today. And, taking Dorothy's place in unveiling the statue will be the youngest of Ernest Gruening's granddaughters, Miss Tiffany Gruening. (Do you know how to do it, honey? Do you know what you're supposed to do? All right, go ahead.—TIFFANY. Do I pull it?—GEORGE. Yes, pull it.—Applause.—You can go back now, honey.)

Please be seated. Tiffany's father, Hunt Gruening, is the only surviving son of Ernest and Dorothy Gruening, who had three sons; and Hunt Gruening, on behalf of the family, will now make a response to the remarks and to the presentation which has occurred here today. Hunt.

HUNT GRUENING. George, distinguished guests and ladies and gentlemen. Many years ago my father once said to me the only truly permanent capital assets that we have in life are the memories of good times. After all, what else really is there? Today the Gruening family, here in force, rich in memories associated with my father, will treasure this proud moment the rest of their lives. The Gruenings, spanning four generations, number today an even dozen persons who proudly bear the name of Gruening, ten of whom are here today. Missing are the oldest and the youngest. And, before I say any more I would like to present to you the Gruenings.

Starting at the top, first generation, of course, is my mother, Dorothy Gruening, the matriarch of the family, who, George has explained, unfortunately could not be here today. She does send her love, however, to all the wonderful friends—Washington and Alaskan friends—she knew here the many years she lived here with my father.

There are two second-generation Gruenings, myself and my Alaskan-born bride of fifteen years, Oline Gruening.

There are eight third-generation Gruenings starting with my eldest son, Clark. Clark, a practicing attorney in Anchorage, now serving a second term in the Alaska State Legislature, has been voted the Gruening most likely to follow in his grandfather's footsteps in the political arena. Clark is here with his wife, Melinda Gruening.

Next come my twin sons, Winthrop and Bradford. Winthrop, the twin over here, is a graduate of the U.S. Air Force Academy, for many years a command jet pilot, has recently defected from the military to civilian life and the business world, and is here with his wife, Anne Gruening.

Brad, who lives in Juneau, Alaska, and has been associated with the fishing and construction industries in Alaska.

[13]

Proceeding on down, next is my oldest daughter, Kimberley. Kimberley, a sixth-grader, is involved in 4–H, horseback riding, swimming, skiing and gymnastics.

Now comes my son Peter. Peter, a fifth-grader, plays baseball, soccer, rides horseback, skis, swims and collects stamps.

And, now comes Tiffany, who did the unveiling. Tiffany, a second-grader, is also a horseback rider, skis, swims and does ballet.

The only other missing Gruening today is Robert Sanders Gruening, age six months, who is the son of Winthrop and Anne Gruening.

Now that you've met the Gruening gang, I would like to say on their behalf how truly thankful we are to the many individuals who've contributed so much to this proud moment. First and foremost, we owe a great debt of gratitude, I believe, to the sculptor, George Anthonisen. George Anthonisen's talented hands have fashioned an image of my father so lifelike and have so skillfully recaptured the spirit of Ernest Gruening that those of you who were close to him, as many of you here today were, can almost feel his presence with us today. This magnificent work of art is more than just a statue perpetuating the memory of my father. I believe it is truly a monument to the talent and genius of George Anthonisen. And, I might add parenthetically that the miraculous thing about this masterpiece is that George Anthonisen never had the opportunity to meet my father during his lifetime; he did this entirely from photographs, clips and his readings of my father's works.

I would also like to thank the distinguished persons who've generously given of their time to come and pay homage to my father here today—in particular, Senator Gaylord Nelson, Senator Ted Stevens, Senator Mike Gravel, Congressman Don Young, Miss Reckley, who participated in this program. The music of your kind words in tribute to my father will echo in our ears for many years to come, and we thank you for this.

Perhaps the unsung hero of this whole affair is the man who

has worked the longest with the least recognition, the Executive Director of the Alaska State Council on the Arts, Mr. Roy Helms. Roy, would you take a bow.

Roy has mothered this whole project from the very beginning over a year ago and has performed such varied tasks as staging a nationwide competition among sculptors and then flying to Issaquah to personally uncrate the seven busts of the competing finalists. I think the success of this whole project and the magnificence of the end product is due largely to this capable handling. If any of you ever needs a statue for a friend or a relative, see Roy Helms. I recommend him highly.

And, finally, we are forever indebted to the people of Alaska, who, through their State Legislature, not only selected my father for this great honor but also passed the enabling legislation which funded it.

And, in a larger sense we are also indebted to the people of the United States, who, through Congress, originally established this gallery of greats.

And, now one final personal thank you to a very special person. Pop, wherever you are, thanks for being my father. It was really great.

GEORGE SUNDBORG. Those of you who knew Ernest Gruening—and I think that encompasses practically everybody in this room—would have to admit that Hunt is his father's son in many ways—in his eloquence and in his sincerity.

When Senator Gruening first stood for re-election in 1962 he was up against a very tough opponent, a young lawyer from Anchorage named Ted Stevens, and it was only with tremendous difficulty that the Senator and I, who was his campaign manager, managed to overcome the threat. The people of Alaska have elected Ted Stevens as a Senator, and he is now the distinguished senior Senator from Alaska. He has, I know, won the confidence, the appreciation and the affection of the citizens of our state. Senator Stevens.

[15]

Senator Ted Stevens.

SENATOR STEVENS. Thank you very much, George. We welcome the Gruening family and all of the friends of Ernest Gruening, for it is with great pride that we add the statue of Senator Ernest Gruening to this Statuary Hall collection. Senator Gruening's memory will stand as an inspiring symbol and a legacy of our state for all Americans.

Like Alaska's land, Ernest Gruening's spirit was heroic in proportion and passion. Like Alaska's life, Ernest Gruening combined a pioneer's vision with the perseverance to surmount overwhelming obstacles to achieve great goals. And, like Alaska, Ernest Gruening was really larger than life; he was extraordinary, awesome, raw, vital, tenacious, honest and most majestic.

He dedicated his life to caring for and curing the ills and injustices of society, climaxing his career as midwife to a state; as a journalist, one of the first to prohibit identification of individuals by race in his news stories; as an author whose "Mexico and Its Heritage" was recognized by the award of the Order of the Aztec Eagle, the Mexican government's highest decoration, and as a crusading administrator who labored to combat Puerto Rico's poverty problems.

Then, as Governor of our Territory of Alaska, Ernest Gruening waged an unrelenting war against discrimination of Alaska's Natives. He turned to our state's vast resources for revenues for improved schools and public services. He stimulated expanded air and highway transportation systems, and he used all of his journalistic skills to champion our cause of Alaska statehood. In his book "The State of Alaska" he presented our case to the nation, based upon historic fact. And, he persuaded Edna Ferber to write "Ice Palace" to popularize our cause in fiction. And, as you have heard from his good friend Gaylord Nelson and others, he became a tenacious lobbyist and truly one who, along with Bob Bartlett, as our first United States Senators, could be called the father of Alaska statehood.

And he was at seventy-one fully qualified to represent the youngest state in our nation. He served his constituents, and he served his conscience. He did not compromise either. His commitment and his vision continued undiminished as a Senator. He championed Hawaii statehood, and we're pleased to see Hawaii's Senator here today. He advocated expanded federal programs for family planning, as Gaylord said. He pressed for civil rights legislation, and along with Wayne Morse, as you've heard, he opposed the Gulf of Tonkin resolution.

So, Alaska did give America a national Senator. But, above all, as we all know, Ernest Gruening was a Senator of and for Alaska. Even after he left office, up to the time of his death, he joined us here in the Capitol to continue to fight for Alaska's progress and our right of self-determination. He appreciated Alaska's environment and understood Alaska's need to balance environmental protection with economic progress. These are his words that he wrote:

"In general, I am on the side of the concerned environmentalist and consider myself not only a conservationist but a fervent one. But where I disagree with my fellow conservationists, whom I class as extremists, is that their concern omits the essential part of the problem—the human element. . . . Man requires a habitat, too, and without a viable economy does he have one? Conservation and development can and must be reconciled: we need both."

He knew that a legislative act alone cannot make a territory a state. Progress, as Ernest Gruening's life proved, results from actions of conscience, not from acts of Congress. We became a state because the Alaskan people wanted to join their identity and their destiny with America's future. We will be a full member of this union as federal officials realize we are a state. In the tradition of Ernest Gruening we must have the candor to assert and the courage to exercise our rights as a state.

On behalf of Alaskans, may I say that this statue honors our statehood as Ernest Gruening's spirit honors our state. Senator Ernest Gruening was a truly great American; he earned the right to stand forever here in the United States Capitol. And, as George mentioned, as a former opponent I want to take this occasion to welcome Ernest Gruening back home to the Senate.

GEORGE SUNDBORG. Ted Stevens is truly an Alaska boy who made good. I should have mentioned in introducing him that he is the Minority Whip of the United States Senate, a great honor which has come to our state.

As if it wasn't tough enough running against Ted in 1962, the next time Ernest came up in 1968, he then being 81 years old, he was opposed by an up and coming young man who had been the Speaker of the House of Representatives of the State Legislature, and on this occasion Ernest was defeated—the only time he was ever defeated in a political campaign. The winner, who will be our next speaker, is the junior Senator from Alaska, Mike Gravel.

SENATOR GRAVEL. Thank you very much, George. And, Hunt, you're most eloquent, beautifully eloquent.

I think it's no small coincidence that we should be here to dedicate this statue today, and standing right next to the statue, is the Magna Carta, a facsimile of the Magna Carta. I can't think of an individual, a human being, who so epitomized what the Magna Carta set in motion—a desire for the realization of freedom among human beings on this planet. And, certainly if the life of Ernest Gruening was dedicated to anything it was truly dedicated to that.

I first met Governor Gruening, as he was called at the time, in 1958–59, and worked in his campaign when he first ran for the Senate. I was what you'd call a protege. I was a very strong admirer of him. I was flattered by his recognition of me and by his association, his desire to stay involved with what were the younger elements of the Democratic Party at that time. I worked in his '62 campaign, helping him to best my colleague here in the Senate.

What drew me to him was the fact that he was a giant of a man. It was a real personal experience just to be associated with him. I used to look forward to the contacts when I'd be able to drive him to a meeting and then sit there and listen to him discourse on various issues—the learning process that a younger politician was able to have at the feet of somebody who was such a giant.

I can recall him confessing once that economically statehood didn't make any sense at all. And, of course, it was the good fortune of oil in '57 that brought about the continuing faith that those people had in the face of no economics that truly did bring about the statehood in a timely fashion.

I admired probably most of all the fact that Ernest Gruening was a great internationalist. He truly looked upon himself as not a citizen of Alaska or of the United States but truly as a citizen of the world, a citizen of the human race. And, I happen to think that that's the highest form of citizenship.

We were friends, and as happens so frequently in the body politic, friendship turned to competition. I ran against Ernest Gruening—not against the man that I respected and truly loved but I ran against a person who occupied an office. And, I, probably more than any other human being, can disagree with George Sundborg and say that Ernest Gruening was not defeated in any electoral contest. Ernest Gruening was defeated by time, as time will defeat us all. That was the only defeat he suffered.

Ernest Gruening had the education of an aristocrat; he had the impulses of a humanist, and he had the vision and energy of a pioneer. It's that last attribute, his pioneering spirit, that so tied him to the destiny of Alaska and Alaska to his destiny, because the credit that he showered upon us through his wisdom, through his courage and through his great humaneness I think is something we Alaskans can be proud of. This man will always be great in the Great Land, Alaska. Thank you.

GEORGE SUNDBORG. Thank you, Senator Gravel. I was reminded while Mike was speaking of something that occurred in the final campaign of Ernest Gruening in 1968. There was a saying that was current among young people at that time—never trust anybody over thirty—remember that this was during the Vietnam war when so many young people did oppose our involvement in Indochina. And, in Alaska, groups of students at the University of Alaska and Alaska Methodist University, our two institutions of higher learning, adapted this saying, and they would say, "Never trust anybody over thirty unless he's also over eighty."

Like four or five other states, Alaska, while it has two Senators, has only one member of the House of Representatives because of our relatively small population. And, the man who is Alaska's Congressman, who has to carry the whole load over in what those who serve in the Senate call the other body, is the Honorable Don Young, who will now speak.

CONGRESSMAN YOUNG. Thank you, George. As the only Congressman, many times when I appear on the podium with the two Senators there's little left to be said. But, I can say it's quite a privilege today to honor this great man, this great Alaskan, Ernest Gruening, the Senator for Alaska. The Gruening family has a right to be proud. This man brought great distinction to the State of Alaska and to the nation as an individual. He also, in an indirect way, is responsible for my being here today honoring him.

He was a great promoter of the resources of the State of Alaska, as our Good Senator Stevens has mentioned. One of his promotions was the Rampart Dam, which would have covered eleven and a half million acres of one of the greatest areas in this great state of ours, making the largest man-made lake in the world. This individual speaking to you now happened to be in the middle of that lake and would have had approximately one-hundred and thirty-five feet of water over my head if it had been built. So, I became an adversary, trying to explain why I thought the project was wrong. In doing so I had the privilege and the honor of meeting a true statesman. From that time on, although I disagreed with him, I held him in the highest regard. He was truly a great Alaskan who accepted individual, independent Alaska thinking, and that was the reason he was able to lead us.

Today, as Senator Stevens has mentioned, Senator Gruening rejoins this congressional body in which he served this great nation and, the greatest state in the union, Alaska. Welcome, Senator.

GEORGE SUNDBORG. Thank you, Representative Young. I think everyone will be relieved to hear that our program is almost over. Before announcing the final item on the program I want to say to you that everyone here is invited after the ceremony to attend a reception which will be held in Room S–207. I am told that the way to get there is to go to the end of the hall toward the Senate side and make two immediate right turns. And, you will find there some Alaska salmon, some Alaska king crab and, I believe, some champagne.

Now, we will close this happy day on which Ernest has joined so many other distinguished men in the Capitol by hearing the U.S. Army Band play a song which always brings tears, for some reason, to the eyes of Alaskans—I know it does to me—and some of you who haven't lived in Alaska may not have heard it before. We think it's a truly beautiful song called "The Alaska Flag Song."

Acknowledgements

David Lloyd Kreeger, President
National Symphony Orchestra Association

Celia Niemi
Office of Senator Ted Stevens

David Gray
Office of Senator Mike Gravel

Dianne Church and Torrey Irving
Office of Representative Don Young

Gladys Reckley, President
Alaska State Society

Toni Friedman
Staff Attorney, Senator Gruening

Roy Helms, Executive Director
Alaska State Council on the Arts

Co-hosts of the Reception
Engstrom Brothers Company
Icicle Seafoods, Inc.
Kootznoowoo, Inc., of Angoon
Western Airlines

The National Symphony Brass Quintet
David Bragunier/David Flowers/Harrison Bowling
Daniel Carter/John Marcellus

Ernest Gruening

Ernest Gruening, destined to be elected a United States Senator from the nation's least populous state—a state which, be it noted, he played a major role in bringing into being—spent his boyhood in America's largest city.

He was born February 6, 1887, in New York City, the only son of Dr. Emil Gruening, an eminent ophthalmologist, and Phebe Fridenberg Gruening. His father had left his native East Prussia at 19 in time to fight as a Union soldier in the Civil War in his adopted country. His mother's family had emigrated to America earlier from the same small village. Phebe was Dr. Gruening's second wife, the first having been her elder sister, who died in childbirth.

It will be recorded here that the family name is pronounced GREENing and that Ernest was given a middle name, Henry, which he despised and ever afterwards refused to use or acknowledge either whole or by the initial.

Senator Gruening once told me that his maternal grandfather, Fridenberg, decided because of encroaching urbanization that he had to move his farm from lower Manhattan to a location farther north on the island. He considered buying a piece of land one of whose corners was at what eventually became Fifth Avenue and 42nd Street but decided against it as being too far out of town.

The Gruening family was bilingual. In his autobiography, a remarkable book entitled *Many Battles* (Liveright, 1973), Ernest Gruening reports that his first language was German which understandably was soon overwhelmed by the English spoken all around him. A third language was soon to be added.

[25]

When he was only seven Ernest went to Europe with his mother and three sisters and, in fulfillment of a belief of his father that all well bred children should learn to speak French while young enough to do so without accent, was enrolled in the Petit Lycee Condorcet in Paris. Fifteen months spent in Europe on this first stay abroad was climaxed by a grand tour of the continent for which Dr. Gruening and Ernest's half-sister, born of the first marriage, joined the rest of the family.

Back in America young Ernest was enrolled in the Drisler School in the fall of 1895. Three years later he transferred to Sachs's Collegiate Institute and in 1902 to the Hotchkiss School in Lakeville, Conn. Summers were spent in additional trips to Europe or on the coast of Massachusetts. One additional educational influence of his youth which Senator Gruening frequently mentioned as being important was Sunday classes conducted by the Society for Ethical Culture.

In the fall of 1903, having passed the entrance examinations, Ernest at the age of 16 entered Harvard College. His class was extended an official welcome by a Harvard senior, the president of the *Crimson,* an attractive young man named Franklin Delano Roosevelt. Others who were at Harvard while he was, and whose acquaintance he made, included Heywood Broun, Walter Lippmann, T. S. Eliot, Harlow Shapley, Robert Edmund Jones, Maxwell Perkins, Earl Derr Biggers, Waldo Pierce, Harper Sibley, Winthrop W. Aldrich and George Whitney.

Ernest said 65 years later that he failed to take advantage of the great opportunities which Harvard offered. His scholastic achievements were mediocre and his extracurricular activities, which included playing on the Harvard chess team, by his own account negligible. But he occupied a room which once housed Ralph Waldo Emerson and enjoyed the companionship of what his friend, Felix Frankfurter, called Harvard's finest feature, "the fastest, the most brilliant of any of the colleges' student bodies."

It had always been taken for granted in the family that Ernest would follow in his father's footsteps and in 1907 he entered

Harvard Medical School. Dutifully he obtained his M. D. in 1912. During his internship he delivered 11 babies, he once told me, but he never practiced medicine as a profession. Instead he went into journalism.

He had written a few drama reviews for the Boston *Traveler* and took his first full time job as a cub reporter on the Boston *American*. Later that same year, 1912, he moved to the Boston *Evening Herald,* advancing to copy desk editor, rewrite man and editorial writer before being appointed managing editor of the Boston *Evening Traveler* in 1914.

A few years earlier while playing tennis Ernest had met a girl who was watching the match. She was Dorothy Elizabeth Smith of Norwood, Mass. Courtship followed and in 1914 they were married.

Always a crusading editor, Gruening got crosswise of his own publisher in connection with stories linking Boston's corrupt and colorful mayor, James Michael Curley, with leading commercial interests. When an apology for an editorial was ordered by the publisher the young editor resigned and took his name off the masthead.

After a year spent as city editor, editorial writer and managing editor of the expiring Boston *Journal* Gruening was invited by Frank Munsey to spend a period observing operations at his New York *Sun* so as to advise him what was wrong with that newspaper. When Gruening became convinced that all that was wrong was Munsey's own imperious meddling with the publication of the news and told him so their association was terminated.

In 1916 Gruening took his first job with the federal government, helping to organize a new Bureau of Imports for the War Trade Board, moving the family to Washington for the first time.

The Gruenings had three sons, Ernest Jr., born in 1915, Huntington Sanders, 1916, and Peter Brown, 1923. The eldest died at the age of 12 of the consequences of a middle ear infection. A second almost unbearable sorrow came to the Gruenings in

1955 when Peter for reasons which were unfathomable took his own life in far away Australia.

A year's contract to serve as managing editor of the New York *Tribune* was cut short by a not uncharacteristic refusal by Gruening to bend the truth to fit the policies of that newspaper's powers that were. He won in court the balance of his year's salary. He was coming to be known as a journalist of uncompromising integrity.

The United States was by then at war with Germany. Gruening entered the Field Artillery Officers Training School in 1918 and served in the Forty-fifth Training Battery until the armistice.

Back in New York he was engaged to help convert the Spanish language weekly newspaper *La Prensa* into a daily. In this effort he dealt with all the many aspects of newspaper publishing which lay beyond the news and editorial rooms—mechanical, financial, advertising, circulation and coping with labor unions.

In 1920 Gruening was invited by Oswald Garrison Villard, owner and editor of *The Nation*, to become its managing editor and subsequently editor, a post he held until 1923. While there he edited *These United States* (Books for Libraries, 1923), an overview of our society which some of his colleagues in the literary world joined him in writing.

A deepening interest in Latin America which began with an attack *The Nation* mounted against our policy of "gunboat diplomacy" led eventually to further service in government and indirectly to the part of the world, Alaska, where Gruening would find his ultimate career.

One of the first fruits of this interest, Gruening's second book *Mexico and Its Heritage* (Century, 1928), followed extensive travels and studies in what its author frequently referred to as his favorite foreign country. To pursue these studies he became fluent in a fourth language, Spanish.

Along the roundabout road to Alaska Gruening won libel suits against Col. Robert R. McCormick of the Chicago *Tribune* and William Randolph Hearst of the Hearst Newspapers for mistakenly attributing the Gruening zeal for international justice to his having been a paid agent of, in the first instance, subversive German, and in the second, Mexican revolutionary, interests.

He also entered actively into domestic politics for the first time to serve as director of publicity for Senator Robert M. LaFollette's unsuccessful campaign for the presidency on the Progressive Party ticket in 1924. He was on the winning side in the second campaign of national interest in which he engaged, Fiorello H. LaGuardia's bid to become the reform mayor of New York City in 1933.

Gruening moved for a time to a new state, Maine, to start a new anti-establishment newspaper, the Portland *Evening News,* whose obsessing crusade throughout his editorship was to expose and do battle with the utility empire of Samuel Insull. A byproduct was Gruening's third book *The Public Pays* (Vanguard, 1931), a popularization and synthesis of the Federal Trade Commission's investigation of the private power industry.

While a resident of Maine from 1927 to 1932 Gruening participated in a popular folly and like so many others became one of its victims. Lured by examples of easy profits in the stock market, he invested the $50,000 he had inherited from his father and lost it all.

Returning to *The Nation* in 1932 he soon accepted an assignment from the new President, Franklin Roosevelt, to serve as the adviser to the U. S. delegation to the 7th Inter-American Conference at Montevideo in 1933 when the new "good neighbor" policy was presented and avidly embraced by the Latin American nations.

There was but one more detour on the long trail to Alaska. In 1934 he was invited by J. David Stern, the owner of two other liberal daily newspapers, to become editor of his newly purchased New York *Evening Post*. Although Gruening had been promised a free hand he was startled after a few months to learn that the publisher had intervened with the Attorney General to forestall impeachment of a corrupt judge who it turned out had done him some favors. When the indignant Gruening faced Stern with this the publisher commented airily, "Oh, you've got to allow me a few fat cats."

"What I should have said to him I didn't think of until later," Senator Gruening told me half a century later. "I should have said I didn't realize I was working in a cat house." They parted company.

In 1934 President Roosevelt asked Gruening to join his administration as director of a newly created Division of Territories and Island Possessions within the Department of the Interior. Obviously it was because of his demonstrated interest and expertise in matters Latin American that he was tapped for this important assignment. But in addition to Puerto Rico and the Virgin Islands the territorial components of the new director's responsibilities included Hawaii and Alaska.

As fate befell, the only specific assignment the President gave Gruening in introducing him at a Hyde Park conference to his new duties related to the problem of Alaska settlement and development. Mr. Roosevelt asked Gruening and Harry Hopkins, the WPA administrator, who also was present, to relocate a thousand or more failed farmers from Minnesota, Michigan and Wisconsin on empty land in the northern Territory. The widely publicized Matanuska Valley resettlement project resulted from this.

To his surprise Gruening discovered a year later that the President in creating a Puerto Rican Reconstruction Administration, the plans for which the new director had drafted, had named him as administrator. Much of his time over the next few years were spent in trying to get agriculture and industry in the impoverished Caribbean Territory on a sound basis.

Ernest Gruening made his first trip to Alaska in 1936, soon becoming acquainted with problems very different from those of Puerto Rico but no less vexing. A second official visit in 1938 increased his interest in the Territory and its future.

In 1937, ranging out from Hawaii and visiting two U.S. island possessions, Guam and American Samoa, which were then under naval rather than civilian administration, a small nautical party under Gruening made a quiet reconnaissance of uninhabited islands in the Pacific which might furnish refueling facilities for flying clippers winging from Hawaii to Australia and New Zealand. The following year an American expedition organized by the Division of Territories and Island Possessions landed on Canton and Enderbury islands in the Phoenix group and claimed U.S. sovereignty. This was vigorously protested by the British who had historic claims, but who subsequently agreed to a condominium which was to last for 50 years. Pan American Airways developed Canton as its only stop on flights between Honolulu and Auckland or Sydney.

In 1939 Gruening's division was drafted by the State Department and the military for a similar purpose involving Antarctica. The United States Antarctic Service which Gruening organized brought ships from three widely separated areas of the northern hemisphere, under hush hush conditions, to land colonists at several points in Antarctica in order to lay a U.S. claim. That purpose having been served, they were withdrawn during World War II. A large icefield in Antarctica was named Gruening Glacier by the expedition.

Against his inclination and recommendation, Ernest Gruening was appointed Governor of Alaska by President Roosevelt in 1939. He felt an Alaskan should be appointed. But Secretary of the Interior Harold L. Ickes, with whom Gruening had been feuding for several years, enthusiastically seconded the President's suggestion. Thus at age 52 Gruening moved to Juneau and found his lasting career.

That Alaska had many problems has been mentioned. These were not, as many might suppose, primarily a harsh climate, rugged terrain and great remoteness from most of what going on in the nation. Many problems, as Gruening by now knew, were even more serious than these. They included sparse population, almost a total lack of roads, abject poverty in the more than 50 per cent of the population which was Native—Alaska's appellation for the Eskimo, Indian and Aleut people who were the region's original settlers—no land transportation connection with the rest of the nation, the highest freight rates under the Flag, land which was 99 per cent owned by Uncle Sam and thus not available for development or settlement, almost no small boat harbors or airfields, housing which was inadequate, a fishery which was declining because of overfishing and existence of a device known as the fishtrap.

Such industry as existed, salmon canning and gold mining, was seasonal and controlled by interests which in the main were located outside of Alaska, as were the steamship companies and the few public utilities. Governmentally, the Territorial Legislature was operating within a straightjacket fastened on the Territory by its Organic Act. Alaskans had no basic tax system to support schools or other public systems or services. The federal agencies, which controlled the resources, were characterized by bureaucratic indifference and staffed by men who were itinerants caring nothing for the Territory's progress.

But the new Governor recognized great inchoate strengths also. These included a wealth of natural resources in all the things— land, water, forests, minerals, energy and unmatched scenic magnificence—which the nation would soon be yearning for. Alaska, moreover, possessed an unspoiled environment and was inhabited by hardy people of great energy, skill, spirit and generosity.

The problems were attacked head-on in characteristic Gruening fashion. An Alaska International Highway Commission, of which he was a member, began studies looking toward construction of an overland route to the Territory across Canada. High transportation rates were investigated by regulatory commissions. A beginning was made in bringing tuberculosis, which had ravaged the Native population, under control.

At first Gruening experienced little success in winning enactment of legislative reforms. The entrenched interests held the Territorial Legislature firmly in their grip. So the Governor mounted and led a political revolution. What was dubbed "the

Gruening machine" began to win elections. But it was not until ten years after his arrival that the Governor won a basic tax system. Alaska began to provide the kind of services and build the kind of institutions people would desire if they were going to stay with the country, not as in times past just make a stake and get out.

One of his successful efforts was to remove the pervasive symbols of racial discrimination against Natives which existed throughout the Territory. After years of struggle he succeeded in having the legislature enact an antidiscrimination act. But he attacked the problem directly also, confronting personally many a surprised restaurant or theatre owner to talk him into taking down the "No Natives Allowed" signs. He encouraged qualified Eskimo and Indian candidates to run for the Legislature, appointed the first Natives to Territorial boards and commissions and established polling places in dozens of Native villages where the people had never had a chance to vote before.

Gruening was the wartime Governor in an area which at last became a cockpit of war. Early he recognized Alaska's vulnerability to airborne or seaborne attack. He helped obtain appropriations to establish Army and Air Force bases, build airfields and develop Navy air stations at Sitka and Kodiak. A battle of a different kind was fought to insure that Alaskans would be employed in the construction of these bases and facilities. On the eve of the battle to recapture Attu from the occupying Japanese he traveled to the Aleutians and mingled with the soldiers who were about to mount the attack, bringing from the commanding general thanks for "the untiring support and encouragement you gave my troops that destroyed the Japanese forces on Attu . . . before the fighting was over and exposed yourself to bring hope and encouragement to my soldiers."

One of his foremost wartime achievements was to organize the Alaska National Guard, including a Territorial Guard whose membership was made up primarily of sharpshooting Native huntsmen from villages stretching from Metlakatla to Barrow.

[33]

Much of the defense buildup occurred in Alaska after World War II, in the cold war era, when the nearness of the potential enemy was only too easy for Alaskans to perceive. Often against official—and even military—complacency, the persistent Governor fought for the appropriations needed to make Alaska secure.

Gruening made many enemies, but he survived. He overcame calculated opposition to his confirmation by the U.S. Senate when he was nominated for a second four-year term by President Roosevelt and for a third by President Harry Truman.

Early in his career as chief executive Gruening discerned that Alaska's problems could never be surmounted piecemeal. They were too numerous. There was a single over-all solution, he felt, one which would cut the Gordian Knot and with that blow both insure adequate attention from Washington and place government at home in the hands of the residents of Alaska. Its name, of course, was Statehood.

Statehood was not easy to sell to Alaskans. Powerful opponents, notably the canned salmon industry, which feared turning regulation of the fisheries over to a State whose people did as their first act abolish the hated fish trap, long persuaded residents that Statehood would bring taxation which would be ruinous. But Gruening gradually won support. A referendum held in 1946 showed Alaskans favoring Statehood by a margin of 9,630 to 6,822.

By the time Alaskans held a Constitutional Convention and drafted a widely acclaimed State Constitution which was ratified in 1956 Gruening had been succeeded by a Republican Governor who was not keen for Statehood. But the same convention provided for election of two provisional "U.S. Senators" and a "U.S. Representative" to carry the Statehood fight to the Congress. Gruening was one of the three Alaskans elected for this role.

Congressional action on an Alaska Statehood bill was completed on June 30, 1958, and election of the first set of congressional and state officials set for November 25 of that year. Ernest Gruening was by that time 71 years old. Although nominated in the primary he ran far behind the attractive young Republican who served as Alaska's last appointed Governor. The campaign was uphill all the way. The very economic development he had espoused and helped make possible had brought thousands of new people to the Territory, tripling the population which existed when Gruening was first appointed. Many of the newcomers had never heard of him, as he had been out of the governorship for more than five years. But with characteristic energy, intelligence and determination Gruening stumped the Territory in its final months before Statehood. Reinforcements were brought up from what Alaskans had begun to call "the Lower 48", Vice President Richard M. Nixon to urge election of the Republican candidate and Massachusetts Senator John F. Kennedy, just emerging on the national scene, to support Gruening and others running with him on the Democratic ticket. When the votes were counted, Gruening had reversed the primary result and won, 26,045 to 23,464.

Alaska was admitted as the 49th State on January 3, 1959, and Gruening and E. L. "Bob" Bartlett sworn in as its first U.S. Senators on convening of the 86th Congress on January 7. Ralph J. Rivers took office that same day as Alaska's first U.S. Representative.

In a keynote address he had been invited to give at the Alaska Constitutional Convention in 1955 and in a book which he entitled prophetically *The State of Alaska* (Random House, 1954) Gruening had laid out in agonizing detail the wrongs, slights and grievances which Statehood was expected to overcome and set right. Now as a U.S. Senator he was in a position, along with his Alaska colleagues, to propose and fight for the legislative and fiscal changes which would make the 49th State veritably equal to the others.

Senator Gruening was sponsor or cosponsor of much legislation dealing with the smooth transition of Alaska from territorial to state status. He was also active in obtaining the enactment of legislation, and the related appropriations, for accelerated highway construction and waterpower development in Alaska. His early years in the Senate were devoted primarily to these long overdue undertakings.

[35]

By lot he drew a term of four years' duration. In 1962 he won reelection for a full six-year term. After the tragic Good Friday earthquake of 1964 which took 124 lives and destroyed large sections of Anchorage, Seward, Kodiak, Valdez and other Alaska communities he took the lead in urging successfully the most generous possible federal relief and reconstruction programs for Alaska.

Similarly, after a destructive flood of the Chena River at Fairbanks in 1967 he persuaded the Public Works Committee, of which he was a member, to hold hearings which led to adoption of a Chena River flood control project designed to prevent such floods in the future.

Along with his busy life as a U.S. Senator, he was able to continue writing and lecturing. Additional books included *An Alaskan Reader* (Meredith, 1967), *The Battle for Alaska Statehood* (University of Alaska Press, 1967) and, with coauthor Herbert W. Beaser of his Senate staff, *Vietnam Folly* (National Press, 1968).

Those who know and remember Senator Gruening primarily for his opposition to U.S. involvement in the war in Vietnam, or even Alaskans who knew of him first when he arrived on that Last Frontier, should be aware that he was a man of many and varied careers who had already spent more than four-fifths of a long and active life of accomplishment before he went to the Senate and three-fifths of that life before he set foot in Alaska.

But nationally his lasting renown will undoubtedly rest on his determined stand against the war in Indo-China. He was only one of two Senators to vote against the Gulf of Tonkin Resolution which gave President Lyndon Johnson virtually a free hand in prosecuting the war against North Vietnam, the other being Senator Wayne Morse of Oregon. Senator Gruening, in nearly daily speeches over the years from 1964 until the end of his service, inveighed against U.S. involvement in that war, saying repeatedly that it should not be our war and that all Vietnam was not worth the life of one American boy.

As Chairman of a subcommittee of the Senate Government

Operations Committee he conducted landmark hearings on the necessity of population control. He participated in, and much of the time chaired, hearings by a subcommittee of the Interior and Insular Affairs Committee, his other major committee, on proposed Alaska Native claims legislation.

In 1968 Senator Gruening was defeated in the primary election for nomination for a third Senate term. He concluded his Senate service in January, 1969. He spent the balance of his life writing, lecturing and participating, with a vigor and intensity which many found surprising in one of his years, in public affairs. He campaigned nationwide, concentrating on college voters, for Democratic presidential candidate George McGovern in 1972 despite his having collapsed at the national convention in Miami Beach from the symptoms of an intestinal tumor and despite both emergency and subsequent follow-up surgery.

That same year, 1972, he became honorary national chairman of a voluntary citizens' committee formed to seek the impeachment of President Nixon. He was moved not by Watergate revelations, which had hardly surfaced at the time, but by the President's invasion of Cambodia and his apparent insistence on continuing the war in Vietnam.

Although his health declined, Senator Gruening was able to work part time for the Population Reference Bureau as a consultant and to complete his autobiography. Only a few weeks before his death he was speaking vigorously and eloquently to Washington audiences about the deep domestic problems which he felt had befallen the nation as a byproduct of the war in Vietnam which, to his outrage, continued for yet a while.

Ernest Gruening suffered a final attack at his home and died in a Washington hospital a few hours later on June 26, 1974.

It is difficult in such brief scope to describe or epitomize this quite remarkable man. His outstanding characteristic, in my view, was his dogged determination. He felt he could prevail, and time after time proved he could, by simply never giving up trying. With this he combined eloquence as a speaker, a keen memory

[37]

even for the smallest details and obscurest names, and a sharp intellect which had been honed to an edge by a good education and almost unrivalled experience.

With all of this he possessed a rare prescience, an ability to see straight through to the heart of an issue instantly and take a stand which was correct and which, sometimes only in the very long run indeed, would be agreed upon by almost everybody. As a result, on issue after issue, he was found in retrospect to be well ahead of his times.

Those of us who knew him and worked with him over long periods—in my case 35 years—learned he would never let us down. He set high standards for himself and, in general, demanded that others live up to the same. But he was a softie when it came to old friends or persons in need of his help. He was, at least in my experience, an easy and generous man for whom to work.

I think I saw him mellow over the years, particularly after it became necessary for him to run for office, but he never sacrificed an important principle.

Dorothy Gruening, as of this writing, still lives quietly in a rest home at Issaquah, Wash. Hunt Gruening, their only surviving son, has four sons and two daughters, so there is no danger that the line will not be perpetuated. Already there is a Gruening great-grandson.

He was never a gold miner or fisherman, never a homesteader on the last frontier or even an enterprising businessman of the kind that has sought and found fortunes in recent times in the 49th State, but Alaskans generally agree that in Ernest Gruening they found an adopted son well worthy to have his likeness cast in bronze to stand in one of Alaska's two places in the National Statuary Hall collection.

November 1, 1977

GEORGE SUNDBORG,
*Administrative Assistant
to Senator Gruening.*

Left to right: Melinda, Clark, Peter, Oline, Tiffany, Kimberly and Hunt Gruening, George R. Anthonisen, Winthrop, Anne and Bradford Gruening.

[Excerpt from the Anchorage Daily News, July 20, 1977]

An Honor Earned

Each state has two places reserved for its distinguished leaders in Statuary Hall in Washington's Capitol Building, and Alaska is about to place its second statue.

The statue is that of Ernest Gruening, perhaps best remembered nationally as a powerful critic of the Vietnam War. His life spanned many careers—medicine, journalism, diplomacy and politics. He was a territorial governor of Alaska and later became one of its first senators.

It's only fitting that the statue of Ernest Gruening will be joining that of his colleague, the late Sen. E. L. "Bob" Bartlett. Together, they established an effective political team for Alaska that earned the respect and trust of both Alaskans and the national leaders with whom they served.

This week, a resolution passed the Senate allowing that upper body to accept the Gruening statue; a similar resolution now goes to the House. And with that, on Oct. 5, the statue by Pennsylvania sculptor George Anthonisen will be unveiled in the Capitol Rotunda, and Ernest Gruening will be standing with the nation's greatest leaders, a place he richly deserves.

[Excerpt from the Southeast Alaska Empire, October 5, 1977]

Family, Friends and Cronies Dedicate Sen. Gruening Statue

BY MARK PANITCH
Empire Washington Correspondent

WASHINGTON—A massive statue of Alaska's late Sen. Ernest Gruening was unveiled today in the Capitol by one of his youngest grandchildren in a ceremony which was charged with both emotion and irony.

The emotion came in a series of oratorical tributes to Gruening from former administrative assistant George Sundborg, Sen. Gaylord Nelson, D-Wisc., Gladys Reckley, president of the Alaska State society in Washington, and his only living son, Hunt.

The irony came when Alaska's three members of Congress, Sens. Ted Stevens, R, and Mike Gravel, D, and Rep. Don Young, R, rose to accept the statue for the Capitol. All three of them, at different times in their political careers, had opposed Gruening, and that was a common theme in their speeches.

Gruening was governor of the territory of Alaska from 1939–53.

From 1953 until 1958, when he returned to Alaska to run for the Senate, Gruening spent most of his time in Washington lobbying for Alaska statehood.

Sundborg noted that Gruening was already 59 when he was appointed to head the territorial government. "Everyone called him the old man," Sundborg said.

But later, he said, Gruening's age became a point in his favor with some supporters. "During the late 1960s when young people were saying never trust anyone over 30," Sundborg said, "students

[41]

at the University of Alaska were saying: 'Never trust anyone over 30, unless he's also over 80.' "

Sundborg, Nelson and Reckley all made clear references to Gruening's stand against the Vietnam War, with Nelson reminding the audience that Gruening spoke out against the war five months before the Gulf of Tonkin resolution was approved in March of 1964.

Gruening and the late Sen. Wayne Morse, D-Ore., were the only two senators to vote against the resolution.

"The life of one American boy is worth more than that whole putrid mess," Nelson quoted Gruening as saying.

Nelson also reminded the audience that Gruening had supported numerous other unpopular causes during his life, including population control in the 1920's when many states made contraception a criminal offense.

In 1974, a few months before Gruening's death, Nelson said a group of senators nominated him for a Nobel Peace Prize. The nominating letter, Nelson said, pointed out that Gruening has backed a number of unpopular causes, but "we have all learned what he believed was usually right."

Stevens spoke about Gruening's "passion, tenaciousness, and honesty" as representative of the Alaska spirit, but he did not mention Gruening's opposition to the war. Instead, in an obvious reference to the on-going Alaska d–2 lands issue, Stevens quoted Gruening as saying that "conservation and development must be reconciled, we need both."

Gravel spoke about being a "prodigy" of Gruening's and of learning the art of politics at the older man's side. "I was flattered when he paid attention to me," Gravel said.

In 1968, Gravel defeated Gruening in the Alaska Democratic primary after a campaign focused on Gruening's opposition to the Vietnam War and his age.

Gruening's son Hunt offered an emotional remembrance of his father that he ended by gazing up at the life-size statue framed against the Capitol Rotunda, saying "wherever you are, thanks pop."

[42]

[Excerpt from the Washington Star, October 10, 1977]

Gruening, Doctor of Diversity, Earned the Praise

BY JACK W. GERMOND AND JULES WITCOVER

In political Washington, the word "great" is thrown around with abandon to describe some of the champion hacks of our time. But it was invoked with justification in the rotunda of the Capitol the other day at the unveiling of a statue of the late Sen. Ernest Gruening of Alaska.

Gruening began his Senate career at the age of 72, a time when most politicians are hanging up their spikes and retiring on a fat government pension. Before that, he had worked tirelessly for Alaskan statehood and was generally considered its father. And before that he was territorial governor, a newspaper reporter and editor, magazine editor, foreign correspondent, author, historian and diplomat—an incredible record for a man trained to be a doctor.

Hubert Humphrey once called him "the 20th century Benjamin Franklin," but "the 20th century Thomas Jefferson" would have been more like it, so versatile was Gruening.

But it is not his versatility that will win him a place in the history books. Along with the late Wayne Morse of Oregon, his voice was the first in the Senate raised against the Vietnam war. Later, he and Morse in August 1964 cast the only votes against Lyndon Johnson's Gulf of Tonkin resolution that was used to escalate the American involvement in that misadventure.

Defeated for re-election after two terms in 1968, Gruening kept up his fight against the war and, at the age of 85, stumped the country in support of George McGovern's anti-war candidacy in

1972. McGovern was in the audience at the unveiling. So was Sen. Gaylord Nelson of Wisconsin, who Gruening always said should have been president. Nelson said as he stood next to the statue that Gruening, a fighter of many battles, "did not always win, but he never lost by default."

Another speaker was Sen. Mike Gravel of Alaska, who defeated Gruening in the 1968 Democratic primary when the old man's age had made him politically vulnerable. Gravel, seeking to be gracious, said that only time had defeated Gruening. But Gravel was dead wrong: Time never laid a glove on Gruening until cancer finally struck him down.

Once in the last years of Gruening's life, a reporter writing about an anniversary of the Tonkin resolution called on him, expecting to find him infirm and senile. Instead, he found a man aroused to indignation in the mere discussion of Johnson and Vietnam. At one point, he raced upstairs and back down again with a letter Johnson had sent him trying to win him over. His mind was off and running, too, and the interview ended some three hours and a notebook of reminiscences later.

In his last months, Gruening found a cause that captured his passions almost as much as bringing the Vietnam war to an end— the impeachment of Richard Nixon. From his hospital bed in June 1974 he followed the House inquiry by watching two television channels simultaneously, reading the Washington and New York newspapers and the Congressional Record daily. Near the end, a visiting reporter was greeted with an arm-waving, fist-shaking denunciation of the then-beleaguered president. Nixon, he said, should not only be impeached, but convicted of high crimes, thrown out of office, then prosecuted as a citizen, convicted again and jailed as an example that American justice still worked.

Among those at the ceremony in the Capitol was a young man named Norman Jacques, a former member of the Rhode Island legislature who refused to be inducted into the armed forces as a protest against the Vietnam war. Gruening heard about him, went and spoke for him and then raised money for his defense. Others present the other day had similar stories to tell, going back to the days when Gruening quit medicine to be a reporter in Boston and eventually a diplomat under FDR.

Dylan Thomas could well have had Ernest Gruening in mind when he wrote pleadingly to the elderly not to submissively let their lives trickle to an end:

"Do not go gently into that good night;
"Old age should burn and rave at close of day;
"Rage, rage against the dying of the light."

Ernest Gruening was a man who raged in his youth, and in his middle age, and at the close of his days for causes that sometimes were unpopular, but always just. None of that spirit can be captured in a statute in the Capitol. But it will be a reminder for those who were privileged to know this "great" and generous man.

[Article from Argus Magazine, January 6, 1978]

Gruening of Alaska

BY A. ROBERT SMITH

A good feeling surges through me when, walking through Statuary Hall in the Capitol, I encounter my old friend Ernest Gruening or, more correctly, the handsome bronze replica of the little giant from the great state of Alaska, which was dedicated a few weeks ago.

Gruening may be remembered by historians as one of the only two brave senators (Wayne Morse of Oregon was the other) who voted against the Gulf of Tonkin resolution which gave President Johnson carte blanche authority to wage war in Vietnam in 1964.

More important perhaps was Gruening's role as the Tom Paine of Alaska.

If it hadn't been for Gruening, Alaska would still probably be a territory, exploited even more today than in the past because of its fabulous wealth in oil and natural gas reserves, most of it discovered after Alaska became the 49th state.

Bob Atwood, editor of the Anchorage *Daily Times,* and a fellow crusader for statehood, always said Gruening was the one who taught Alaskans how to stand up and fight to throw off the colonial rule of territorialism.

A former magazine editor and newspaperman, Gruening became the pamphleteer of their cause. His books and magazine articles, long after he had left the governorship of the territory, articulated the case for self-government an end to domination, he freely charged, by commercial interests based chiefly in Seattle.

Gruening was not only an activist but probably the most learned man in Alaska—"a Renaissance man with guts," as one admirer put it. Medical doctor, Latin American expert, New Deal office-holder (he and FDR were at Harvard together) and author were some of his earlier distinctions.

[46]

It's a shame that Gruening didn't live through the current era of controversy over the disposition of Alaska's vast lands and resources, for he had a vision that might have helped considerably to resolve the squabble over whether to set aside millions of acres in new national parks, wildlife refuges and wilderness areas.

Interior Secretary Cecil Andrus has proposed 92 million acres. Environmentalists want much more and commercial interests, including the Seattle Chamber of Commerce, want to hold it to much less. Congress must settle it during 1978.

Gruening visualized Alaska not as a colony to be exploited for "the lower 48" nor as a vacationland for wealthy adventurers. He said Alaska should become the American Scandinavia, with its own fully developed economy and social lifestyle.

Although a strong liberal, Gruening wanted Alaska's resources to be fully developed, not locked up. And while he railed against the salmon packers, who once represented the most powerful industrial interest in Alaska, it was because he just didn't want them to deplete the fisheries for the benefit of absentee owners.

His philosophy, as I understood it, was that our largest state can support a substantial population if its resources are developed for the benefit of its own citizens rather than outsiders. The big oil strike on the North Slope was on state lands, so the state will benefit handsomely from royalties, and that could lay the financial foundation for the fulfillment of Gruening's dream of an American Scandinavia.

If he and his compatriots hadn't succeeded in winning statehood in the Fifties, the heavy oil extraction from Alaska during the Seventies and Eighties might have sucked it dry by the Nineties, leaving Alaska to flounder economically, an icy wasteland instead of a viable, vibrant sector of the nation.

In Statuary Hall, where each state is entitled to two memorials, there are giants (Lincoln, Lee) and pygmies (Sen. Pat McCarran of Nevada, for example).

There never should be any doubt in which rank Ernest Gruening stands.

[47]

George R. Anthonisen, Sculptor

George R. Anthonisen is a sculptor residing in Bucks County, Pennsylvania whose work is recognized and collected throughout the nation.

The major part of Anthonisen's career has been directed toward private and architectural commissions. His style merges a traditional training with his unique understanding of human nature. His subjects, although realistically portrayed, go beyond academic realism. They are expressive of people in contemporary society showing all their conflicting moods and emotions.

Anthonisen was born in Boston, Massachusetts in 1936. His parents were psychoanalysts. He is the middle of three brothers.

He began the study of sculpture in his junior year at the University of Vermont. After graduation, he studied in New York City at The National Academy of Design and The Art Students League. He ended his formal studies at Dartmouth Medical School dissecting cadavers to further enhance his knowledge of anatomy.

Anthonisen feels that living in New York in the sixties played an important role in his growth as an artist. It was at this time that two major issues that confront the world today came into disruptive perspective—civil rights and the issue of United States involvement or lack of involvement in the political affairs of other countries (Vietnam, Biafra). He sees these issues as having an important impact on his work. It was also at this time that Anthonisen met and married his wife Ellen and they had their two children Rachel and Daniel.

In 1971, Anthonisen and his family moved away from New York to Pennsylvania. During the summer of this move, he was selected as sculptor-in-residence at Augustus Saint-Gaudens National Historic Site. It was a three month appointment, but for Anthonisen it was the beginning of what he considers to be his bona fide professional life as a sculptor. Although he had already had two one-man shows, he feels that he was truly inspired while living on the estate of the famed turn-of-the-century sculptor Augustus Saint-Gaudens.

Anthonisen's awareness of Senator Ernest Gruening in the 1960's was that of a removed but kindred spirit relating most specifically to the United States action in Vietnam.

It was not until he started studying Senator Gruening, through his autobiography *Many Battles* that the sculptor realized how many of the Senator's beliefs reflected his own feelings. Indeed, he felt a spiritual bond with the late Senator. Coincidentally, they both came from medical backgrounds and they both had a coming together of christian and jewish cultures in their immediate family structures.

The sculptor's works *Death and Starvation* and *Memorial* are reflections of Senator Gruening's concepts of war and population control. Another issue that has been of significance in Anthonisen's work has been the issue of civil liberties.

Anthonisen feels that Senator Gruening's deepest beliefs were humanitarian—a humanitarian whose first loyalties lay with the United States of America. He feels that Senator Gruening believed, as he does, that humanism is the strength of this country and that it abounds in this country as in no other. If we are to remain strong and continue to grow, we must maintain our sense of decency and humanity at home and abroad with all peoples everywhere.

[50]

[Excerpts from the Philadelphia Sunday Bulletin, October 2, 1977]

Artist Gets Wish for Birthday

BY JUDY TUCKER

Special to The Bulletin

Bucks County sculptor George Anthonisen vowed that he was going to do "something big" before his 40th birthday.

Quite a promise from an artist whose bust of George Gershwin was already part of the permanent exhibit at Carnegie Hall and whose work was owned by countless museums and private collectors including the Gerald Fords.

But Anthonisen kept that vow.

Last year, exactly 53 days before he turned 40, Anthonisen joined the ranks of a handful of distinguished sculptors whose statues of famous Americans are included in a special collection at the Capitol Building in Washington, D.C.

Anthonisen explained his tie-in with this collection as he relaxed in the living room of his home in Solebury, surrounded by his two- and three-foot-high bronze nudes, miniature studies and bas-reliefs. Shortly after the Civil War, Congress voted to invite each state to furnish two statues of its most illustrious citizens for permanent display in the Capitol.

This Wednesday the latest addition to that collection will be unveiled and dedicated. It is Anthonisen's seven-foot statue of the late Ernest Gruening, Alaska's first United States Senator.

The son of a psychoanalyst-father and a child psychiatrist-mother, Anthonisen was born in Boston and grew up showing little interest in sculpture or art "except maybe for whittling knives and guns and drawing pictures of airplanes."

While an undergraduate at the University of Vermont, Anthonisen was looking for an easy course and signed up for a class in sculpture.

[51]

[Photo by Dom Ligato, the Evening and Sunday Bulletin, Philadelphia, Pa.]

Sculptor George Anthonisen attends to his statue of Ernest Gruening.

"It turned out to be a lot of fun," he says now. "So I ended up going on to the National Academy of Design in New York and then to Dartmouth College to dissect cadavers with the med students so I could learn more about anatomy."

In 1971 Anthonisen, his wife Ellen and their two young children moved to Bucks County. Anthonisen's first job was to build a one-room, A-frame, skylighted studio in his wooded back yard.

A recent edition of "Who's Who in American Art" describes the quality of Anthonisen's work as "contemporary realism."

The sculptor calls it "subjective" and "expressionistic." He added that he "attempts to bring out all the different conflictive forces that exist within (each subject) and let those forces interact, without editing out any good or bad."

Ellen Anthonisen puts it another way: "George's work is analytical, perhaps because he grew up in his parents' home . . . his work is powerful in its psychological impact and there's a certain 'gut' about it that people respond to."

Two years ago, Anthonisen heard that the Alaska State Council on the Arts was conducting an open competition: The winning artist would be commissioned to execute a statue of the late state senator for the Capitol, as well as a bust of Gruening for the University of Alaska.

More than 300 artists submitted resumes and photographs of their work. Of that number, seven were selected as "semi-finalists" and each was asked to do a life-size bust of Gruening.

Doing a three-dimensional portrait without having the subject available for sittings wasn't new to Anthonisen. His bust of Gershwin was made years after the musician's death. He had to "read everything about the man and study every available picture of him."

"I did the same thing here," Anthonisen says. "I read Gruening's autobiography; spent $35 for a collection of photographs of him; talked to everybody I could find who knew him, and then started to synthesize all those different aspects."

It took Anthonisen six months to complete the bust and get it shipped off to Alaska.

[53]

On June 8, 1976, he received word that he was the winner.

Anthonisen claims that he is still overwhelmed at the prospect of having a piece of his work "in the archives of the United States . . . which practically makes it a piece of history."

"I feel that I have finally established myself . . . and have sort of 'arrived'," he adds, embarrassed about having to put all of this into words. "It gives one a kind of confidence."

On Wednesday, the Anthonisens, their children and some close friends will go to Washington for the dedication ceremony in the Capitol Rotunda and a champagne brunch that follows.

Will it be a let down for Anthonisen when he returns home afterward?

Not really, he says.

He is already at work on a bust of art patron Joseph Hirshhorn that was commissioned by the Hirshhorn's daughter.

Laws of Alaska, 1975

(Source: SB 82 am H; Chapter No. 186)

AN ACT Authorizing the construction of a life-sized statue of the late Senator Ernest Gruening; and providing for an effective date.

Be it enacted by the Legislature of the State of Alaska:

Section 1. For the purpose of constructing a life-sized statue of the late Senator Ernest Gruening for permanent placement in the National Statuary Hall collection in the Rotunda of the United States Capitol in Washington, D.C., the Alaska State Council on the Arts shall—

(1) work with federal officials to determine what requirements and standards must be met for such a statue; and

(2) select a sculptor to make the statue and negotiate a contract with the sculptor subject to legislative approval by concurrent resolution.

Sec. 2. The commissioned sculptor shall have all details, including the model to be used, approved by Mrs. Dorothy Gruening, and the final product shall also be approved by Mrs. Dorothy Gruening before placement of the statue in the National Statuary Hall collection in the Capitol Rotunda.

Sec. 3. The contract with the sculptor shall include the production of a bust of the late senator taken from the life-sized statue. This bust shall be for presentation to the University of Alaska.

Sec. 4. This Act takes effect immediately in accordance with AS 01.10.070(c).

Approved by Governor: June 25, 1975
Actual effective date: June 26, 1975

Authentication

The following officers of the Legislature certify that the attached enrolled bill, Senate Bill No. 82 am H, consisting of one page, was passed in conformity with the requirements of the constitution and laws of the State of Alaska and the Uniform Rules of the Legislature.

Passed by the Senate June 6, 1975.

CHANCY CROFT,
President of the Senate.

Attest:

BEVERLY KEITHAHN,
Secretary of the Senate.

Passed by the House June 5, 1975.

MIKE BRADNER,
Speaker of the House.

Attest:

IRENE CASHEN,
Chief Clerk of the House.

ACTION BY GOVERNOR

Approved by the Governor June 25, 1975
JAY S. HAMMOND,
Governor of Alaska.

Ninth State Legislature

W. E. "Brad" Bradley
John Butrovich
Genie Chance
Mike Colletta
Chancy Croft
Frank R. Ferguson
George H. Hohman
John Huber
Jalmar M. Kerttula
H. D. "Pete" Meland

Terry Miller
Joseph L. Orsini
Kay Poland
John L. Rader
Bill Ray
Patrick Rodey
Jahn Sackett
Clem V. Tillion
Edward C. Willis
Robert H. Ziegler, Sr.

Nels A. Anderson, Jr.
Helen D. Beirne
Willard L. Bowman
Bob Bradley
Mike Bradner
Fred Brown
Thelma Buchholdt
Samuel R. Cotten
Steve Cowper
Larry T. Davis
Jim Duncan
Richard I. Eliason
Tom Fink
Helen M. Fisher
Oral Freeman
Terry Gardiner
Clark Gruening
Phil Guy
Glenn Hackney
E. J. Haugen

H. M. "Mike" Hershberger
James H. Huntington
Brenda T. Itta
Ramona M. Kelly
Joseph H. McKinnon
Hugh Malone
Mike Miller
Edward F. Naughton
Al Ose
Alvin Osterback
Kathryn Ostrosky
William K. Parker
Charles H. Parr
Leo Rhode
Theodore G. Smith
Keith W. Specking
Susan Sullivan
Leslie E. "Red" Swanson
Richard K. Urion
Tim Wallis

[57]

Senate Concurrent Resolution No. 25

May 16, 1977

Mr. GRAVEL (for himself and Mr. STEVENS) submitted the following concurrent resolution; which was referred to the Committee on Rules and Administration providing for the acceptance of a statue of the late Senator Ernest Gruening presented by the State of Alaska for the National Statuary Hall collection, and for other purposes.

Resolved by the Senate (the House of Representatives concurring), That the statue of the late Senator Ernest Gruening, presented by the State of Alaska for the National Statuary Hall collection, is accepted in the name of the United States, and the thanks of the Congress are tendered to the State of Alaska for the contribution of the statue of one of its most eminent personages, illustrious for his distinguished civic services.

SEC. 2. The State of Alaska is authorized to place temporarily in the rotunda of the Capitol the statue of the late Senator Ernest Gruening referred to in the first section of this concurrent resolution, and to hold ceremonies in the rotunda on that occasion. The Architect of the Capitol is authorized to make the necessary arrangements therefor.

SEC. 3. (a) The proceedings in the rotunda of the Capitol at the presentation by the State of Alaska of the statue of the late Senator Ernest Gruening for the National Statuary Hall collection, together with appropriate illustrations and other pertinent matter, shall be printed as a Senate document. The copy for such document shall be prepared under the direction of the Joint Committee on Printing.

(b) There shall be printed five thousand additional copies of such document which shall be bound in such style as the Joint Committee on Printing shall direct, of which one hundred and three copies shall be for the use of the Senate and three thousand copies shall be for the use of the Members of the Senate from the State of Alaska, and four hundred and thirty-nine copies shall be for the use of the House of Representatives, and one thousand four hundred and fifty-eight copies shall be for the use of the Members of the House of Representatives from the State of Alaska.

SEC. 4. The Secretary of the Senate shall transmit a copy of this concurrent resolution to the Governor of Alaska.

We Alaskans believe—passionately—that American citizenship is the most precious possession in the world. Hence we want it in full measure; full citizenship instead of half citizenship; first class instead of second class citizenship. We demand equality with all other Americans, and the liberties, long denied us, that go with it. To adapt Daniel Webster's famous phrase uttered as a peroration against impending separatism, we Alaskans want "liberty *and* union, one and inseparable, now and forever."

ERNEST GRUENING
From Keynote address to Alaska
Constitutional Convention, 1955

The United States should get out of Vietnam. . . . The war in South Vietnam is not and never has been a U.S. war. . . . I consider the life of one American worth more than this putrid mess. I consider that every additional life that is sacrificed in this forlorn venture a tragedy. Some day—not distant—if this sacrificing continues, it will be denounced as a crime. . . . This is a fight which is not our fight into which we should not have gotten in the first place. The time to get out is now before the further loss of American lives. . . . Let us get out of Vietnam on as good terms as possible—but let us get out.

ERNEST GRUENING
From his first full dress Vietnam
speech in the Senate, March 10, 1964

[60]